10 Most Common Prayer Mistakes...
and How to Avoid Them

by

Gayle Smith Daniels, MSA, MCC

PRESS

Contents

Acknowledgments

First and foremost, I thank God for His inspiration and role in His leading and guiding role in writing this book. I give special thanks to my gifts from God: my dear husband, Marvin Lee Daniels for his continued support and encouragement in all my endeavors; and my loving children, Marissa Denise and Marvin L. Daniels, II.

I also want to thank my pastor, Gary Hawkins Sr., for agreeing to write the forward and his lovely wife, Elder Debbie Hawkins, for her insightful thoughts. I also thank God for the editorial talent, skills and gifts of Beverley Cummings. I truly bless Him for my special friend Cheryl M. Cannon and my mother-in-law, Louise Daniels for their encouragement throughout this project.

Finally, I give special thanks to Minister Donetta Pickett and Michael and Tammy Anderson who constantly prayed for and with me during this endeavor.

Foreword

I believe the body of Christ suffers greatly due to a lack of effective communication with God. We've not been taught the proper way to pray and push for an answer until we hear from God. I believe 70 percent of believers never reach their destiny with God because they don't take the time to inquire from Him their purpose for living. Praying daily to God will elevate an intimate relationship with Him. It does not matter whether you are a new convert or a Christian who has struggled in the past with knowing the proper way to pray, God allows U-turns. God gives us an opportunity to correct common mistakes that's preventing us from prospering in the kingdom.

Gayle Smith Daniels has reminded us that God truly does allow U-turns. God gives us another opportunity to correctly pray effectively to Him. Gayle's book, **"10 Most Common Prayer Mistakes...and How to Avoid Them"** is masterfully written for the 21st century church. She has tapped into a resource that the body of Christ desperately needs. Gayle has simplified effective communication with God by sharing with us how to avoid common mistakes with God during our prayer time.

This book is written and designed to bless your life beyond measures. Every believer and new convert alike should read this book twice a year. If you are struggling with communicating with God or would like to take your prayer life to another level with God, **"10 Most Common Prayer Mistakes...and How to Avoid Them"** will change your life forever.

Pastor Gary Hawkins, Sr.
Voices of Faith Ministries
Stone Mountain, Georgia

Introduction

*G*od wants us to talk to Him. He wants His children to make their requests known. Finally, He desires that we believe in Him that our deepest, Godly desires will be fulfilled.

Prayer is making our request known to Him.

As Christians, many of us pray and talk to God because this is what He commands from us. Jeremiah 33:3 states,

> *"Call upon me, and I will answer thee, and show thee great and mighty things, which thou knowest not."*

Further instruction is given in Luke 18:1,

> *"And he spake a parable unto them to this end, that men ought always to pray, and not to faint."*

Prayer is making our request known to Him and believing through faith that His will is done in our lives. The following are additional reasons we should pray:

- *God commands it;*
- *Prayer honors God;*
- *Prayer helps build a relationship with Him through communion;*
- *Prayer allows us to receive what we need from God;*
- *Prayer helps us to know the heart of the Father and His desires for us;*
- *Prayer allows us to communicate and have a conversation of the heart with the Father;*
- *Prayer allows us to seek and find what God wants in and for our lives based on His commandments;*
- *Prayer provides guidance and direction to challenging situations and circumstances; and*
- *Prayer helps us stay focus on God and in tuned to His will.*

When we pray, our first desire should be for God's will to be done thereafter, our desires to be fulfilled. This type of attitude speaks to the correctness of our mindset. This is why Jesus said in Matthew 6:9-10,

> *"After this manner therefore pray ye:*
> *Our Father which art in heaven,*
> *Hallowed be thy name*
> *Thy Kingdom come*
> *Thy will be done in earth, as it is in heaven."*

This approach signifies the importance Jesus placed on the process and perception of prayer. In Luke 11, God gave us a model for effectively communicating and communing with Him based on this text. We should begin our prayers by acknowledging who God is ...All Knowing, All Wise, All Loving, All Merciful, and All Powerful. He is the King of Kings and Lord of Lords. He is the

Creator of Creation. Before Him there was nothing! Our perceptions and what we believe about Him should provide guidance to our desires as we enter into the Throne of Grace in prayer. From this perception, we know that God is able to provide us with the desires of our heart because of our faith in who He is. Through faith in His will, there is no doubt that we will receive the riches and blessings promised in His word.

Before we can walk in His promises, our hearts must be cleansed from sin daily through the Holy Spirit before we can go before the Lord in prayer. Often, saying a prayer becomes routine and mechanical. We tend to go to God any way we please, often with anger, hatred and even jealousy in our hearts. Yet at the same time, we want Him to bless our unforgiving hearts. This is unacceptable to Him; we must have a proper posture and a clean heart. Having a proper posture deals with the inner man and how we position ourselves. In other words, before going to the Lord in prayer, we must examine ourselves to ensure "self" has been denied. In doing so, we actually seek cleansing from things that exist in our hearts that are not pleasing to the Father. As a result, cleansing and purification manifest in our Spirits as we begin to walk in the will of the Lord.

This means we must search after the will of God first and His Holy Spirit will direct us to receiving exactly what God would have for us to receive. Romans 8:26, states

"Likewise the Spirit also helpeth our infirmities: for we know not what we should pray for as we ought: but the Spirit itself maketh intercession for us with groanings which cannot be uttered."

Romans 8:27 tells us,

"And he that searcheth the hearts knoweth what is the mind

of the Spirit, because he maketh intercession for the saints according to the will of God."

In 1992, during the first few years of my ministry, I spent a lot of time praying for others. I interceded for others regarding healing, deliverance, financial blessings, or anything they desired from the Lord. I thought this was what I was supposed to do. We all need prayer I thought. However, I did not give much thought to the process of my heart-nor theirs. I would pray because someone asked me, not discerning whether our lives were connected with God. I also did not take into consideration the importance of asking God for His will first to get my prayers answered. I would pray for what was desired at the time, irrespective of His will. As a result, I did not grow in God's grace. I did not understand at the time truly the power of prayers and communicating with the Father. Ultimately, the process to receiving is to acquire a renewed mind after God's will, a focused heart after the Father and then pursue after our own desire.

Mistake #1

Misunderstanding the Meaning of Prayer

CHAPTER ONE

*J*esus' disciples not only followed after Him, but they watched Him closely. They had a thirst to learn and be taught by their Master. They must have had a pretty good understanding of the significance of prayer because they asked Him to teach them in Luke 11:1 and Jesus granted their request.

"And it came to pass, that, as he was praying in a certain place, when he ceased, one of his disciples said unto him, Lord teach us to pray, as John also taught his disciples."

In *Merriam-Webster Collegiate Dictionary* communication is defined as "a process by which information is exchanged between individuals through a common system of symbols, signs, or behavior." Within this process, Jesus made His requests, thoughts, feelings and desires known to the Father. Jesus gained strength through His prayers. Prayer to Him was like Gatorade to us. It revitalizes, regenerates, and rejuvenates the body and spirit. This is what prayer should be to us. A common mistake we have is misunderstanding the meaning of prayer. Prayer means to communicate and have a conversation of the heart with the Father. Jesus' disciples witness Him doing so on numerous occasions. They observed the two-way dialogue displayed by Jesus to His Father. They watch Jesus develop a personal relationship with the One they knew was omnipotent and omnipresence.

Prayer is designed to develop and/or enhance our personal relationship with the Father through the Holy Spirit. Sometimes we don't understand or we take for granted the concept of relationship building with Christ. I say this because often we limit our conversations with Him. When we pray, we send up quick prayers that are mechanical and routine at best. Typically, we pray because this is what we have been taught to do and it is out of habit, without purpose. We even fail to bow down to Him on a regular basis. While this is not a sole requirement for prayer, the book of Matthew illustrates every time that someone petitioned Jesus, they bowed down to Him in recognition of who He was. Likewise, our prayers sometimes have no meaning because we seek Him without a clear focus on His will.

We must realize that when we communicate with God, we are acknowledging Him as the Supreme Being. We actually give and receive information to and from the Most High. During prayer, we give our heartfelt thoughts and seek His Sovereign powers of blessings. When we pray, we literally recognize and acknowledge that He has made provision in His Word that we must abide by and He has the ability and is willing to hear our cries and answer prayer requests. God doesn't want His people to come to Him without acknowledging His directives. Therefore, when we pray to our Father, we actually seek to find what He wants in and for our lives based on His commandments. Hence, when we pray, we should not solely look for or focus on what we desire from our flesh. For example, John 15:7, states,

"If you abide in me, and my words abide in you, ye shall ask what ye will, and it shall be done unto you."

Only then will our prayers be answered. The key element to this scripture is *"His Words abiding in us."* In other words, we should ask ourselves whether we are living a life that glorifies God, or seeking Him for personal gain. In this way, we should align ourselves with our Creator to allow His presence to be revealed. As a result, whatever we seek from the Lord should first and foremost be for His benefit and not primarily our own desires.

The essence of prayer helps us to know the heart of the Father and His desires for us. It helps us to know His wishes and commands. We seek God in prayer to get to know Him and commune with Him. In doing so, prayer will provide guidance and direction in challenging situations and circumstances. Prayer will help us stay focus on God and alert to His will as we attempt to know Him better and gain the desires of our hearts. Prayer is making our request known unto Him through faith. God tells us to ask, seek and knock in Matthew 7:7-8. He also states in Matthew 6:33 that we should seek His righteousness first. Then and only then will He bless us with our desires.

"Ask, and it shall be given you; seek, and ye shall find; knock, and it shall be opened unto you; For everyone that asketh receiveth; and he that seeketh findeth, and to him that knocketh it shall be opened."

"But seek ye first the Kingdom of God, and his righteousness; and all these things shall be added unto you."

Seeking after His righteousness is the focal point of these scriptures. It involves agreeing with God and aligning ourselves with His will. Have you ever felt the need to immediately have a problem solved or tell someone something that was burning in your heart? You couldn't wait until you saw that person. That burning sensation to receive an answer or release your heart, is the same feeling you should have about talking and getting to know our Father. Prayer is like telling God, who you recognize as All Powerful, the most important thing you can imagine knowing that He delights in hearing from His child. It is like saying to Him, "I know you are everlasting, the end all beat all, the All Mighty and Wonderful Savior. Therefore, I come to You for YOUR advice and guidance. Lord, I come to YOU because I don't want to mess up and I desire to share with you my heartfelt emotions." The good news is God already knows our heart. He knows whether you are coming to him earnestly in truth or for show as Hypocrites. He truly knows your motives. The word of God says the man who accepts Godly counsel is blessed. It is through His grace of the Holy Spirit that He gives us power to resist evil, wrongdoing and temptation.

It has been my experience that we generally go before the Lord in prayer when there are trials, tribulations, uncertainty and unexpected events in life. While these things draw us to talk more frequently to the Father, He also wants us to come to Him in reverence of His name, for who He is, seeking His will, His Kingdom, and avoidance and deliverance from evil. He not only wants to hear from us when we need material and physical things such as cars, houses, increase wealth, friends or spouses, but He wants our souls to be constantly connected with His. He wants to hear from us on a regular basis regarding how His presence glorifies our lives. He wants His name to be praised. He wants us to have feelings similar to those we have with someone we truly love and adore. For example, do you remember when you first met your true love? You couldn't wait to talk to that person. You talked for hours on end about nothing. You shared your life experiences, the activities of your day and the upcoming challenges that you were to face. Now, think about this for a moment. God wants you to have those same feelings about Him. Have you ever had a relative or someone you consider a close friend or associate who only calls you when they need something? Making matters worse, when they connected with you, everything was about them. I postulate that your response was usually, "they don't pick up the phone or send you an email until it's time to receive." I surely have people like this in my life and it isn't a good feeling. Let's take it a little further. Have you ever thought about how many of us treat our Father this way? Just imagine how He must feel when His children do this. Just imagine how you would feel if He said, "I'm going to hold back your blessings because I only hear from you when you need or want something." Are you one of these types who seldom talk with the Lord and when you do, it's all about yourself? It's all about what you want and not about His desires for your life. I don't believe many of us can say we truly fellowship with the Lord as He expects and commands. How often do you commune with our Lord and Savior? How often do you go to Him with praise in your heart? How often do you seek His ways and His directions for your life? How often do you tell Him how much you need and want His presence to manifest in your spirit? Is it only during tragedy or uncertainty? What a terrible thing to envision. The good news is, God blesses us even when we show Him He is less than a friend. Perhaps at this moment we should acknowledge our sin of praylessness and begin to talk with the Lord and seek forgiveness.

Talking with God should be a pleasure each and every day, to be repeated many times per day. We should abide by I Thessalonians 5:17 and be like the Apostle Paul and pray without ceasing. Prayer is not just asking God for what we want from Him, but it is sharing our innermost feelings, thoughts, and desires, while giving praise unto His name. God has made provision for His people to earnestly commune with Him. He set a communication model in place so that His people may build a closer relationship with Him through His Son, Christ Jesus, and the Holy Spirit. When we pray, we fellowship with God and welcome His presence in our lives wholeheartedly. While prayer is asking and receiving, our first priority when we pray is for His will to be done in everything. When we are unsure of His will, we should seek it until we find it through the Holy Spirit. We should continue to talk with Him without ceasing. However, our sinful hearts must be cleansed daily through the Holy Spirit before we go before the Lord in prayer because Scripture teaches us that God doesn't listen to sinners. John 9:31 states:

"Now we know that God heareth not sinners: but if any man be a worshiper of God, and doeth his will, him he heareth."

Therefore, to please God and effectively communicate with Him, we must have a righteous heart and obedient spirit. As a result of pleasing the Lord and following His commandments, not only will God hear our prayers, but He promised to answer. God has an obligation to do so. We must maintain a standard of righteousness, otherwise our prayers are hindered. We must stop the saying "practice what you preach," and begin to incorporate a motto of "preach what you practice." In other words, abide by James 1:22 which states,

"But be doers of the word, and not hearers only, deceiving your own selves."

Prayer causes us to experience joy and tranquility. We find the love of Christ abiding in our spirits and souls. Prayer brings about a change of heart and manifests a spirit of obedience in our souls.

When we pray, we avoid hatred and obtain love and humility. Prayer gives strength to the weak, manifests love for enemies, and creates a humble spirit toward persecutors. We are able to break strongholds of unrighteousness and become filled with the loving grace and peace of God. When we pray and discern the will of God, mountains move and the experience of life become magnified. When we pray God opens up the windows of heaven with blessings unimaginable. Prayer and communion with God bring peace that surpasses all understanding. It creates clean hearts and renewed mindsets and spirits. It makes God's promises known so that everyone can receive them. Prayer will make you want to give away your last dime without worrying about tomorrow because you know your Father in heaven will make a way out of no way. When we bow down and fellowship with the Lord we quickly forgive others and take ownership for our wrongdoings. Since God is omnipotent, prayer will deliver you from bondage and keep you on the path of righteousness to resist temptation. Prayer means to abide in the Lord and allow His word to abide in you for His glorification and the edification of the human soul, mind and body. God wants you to take time from each given day to fellowship with Him, and to develop and create oneness with Him. This means we must daily, consistently and meaningfully, take on the acts of Apostle Paul and pray. We must be zealous and fervent in our prayers to receive God's overflowing power for the many desires of our hearts. Won't you begin today?

Mistake #2

Wrong Reasons,
Wrong Motives

CHAPTER TWO

Sometimes in life, we pray for the wrong reasons with the wrong motives. This is another common prayer mistake because we get sidetracked with our motives and seek after things that are not pure nor worthy of God's blessing. Ask yourself the following questions:

1. Have you ever wanted something because someone else had it?
2. How often do you really consider why you desire a certain items or person?
3. Have you prayed for something that led to pride, injustice or selfishness? Or did your desire produce humbleness and a submissive spirit?
4. How often do you check your motives before making a request to the Father?

In James 4 we're guided to ask for the right motives. Verse 3 states,

"Ye ask, and receive not, because ye ask amiss,
that ye may consume it upon your lusts."
Verse 3:16 states, *"For where envying and strife is,*
there is confusion and every evil work."

In other words, we hinder our blessings because we allow wrong motives to accompany our prayer requests. For that reason, we must prepare our hearts and minds toward the goodness of God before we pray. He commands us to study and speak His words in our prayers to obtain His blessings. To achieve this, we must constantly mediate on our source...the word of God. We should seek understanding when we aren't clear on His will to ensure that our spirit is aligned with His purposes and promises. The word of God says in Romans 8:27,

"And he that searcheth the hearts knoweth what is the mind
of the Spirit, because he maketh intercession for the saints
according to the will of God."

In our society, it is easy to have the wrong motives when petitioning the Lord in pray. Again, in the New Testament of the Book of James we are warned of the consequences of doing so. James 4:3 states,

"Ye ask, and receive not, because ye ask amiss, that ye may
consume it upon your lusts."

If we ask for things to please ourselves or impress others, we have the wrong motives. James 4:3 explains that when we ask and do not receive it is because we ask with wrong motives knowing what we desire to receive will be spent on our pleasures. Additionally, Matthew 6:5 teaches that prayer should not be for show or boasting. It states,

"And when thou prayest, thou shalt not be as the hypocrites are: for they love to pray standing in the synagogues and in the corners of the streets, that they may be seen of men. Verily I say to you, They have their reward."

Therefore, when we pray, we should seek after things that please God rather than ourselves. God knows our desires and He also knows that we will sometimes not understand Him.

I remember a time when I was earnestly seeking God's face, praising Him every chance I had, and praying for His will to continuously be done in my life. Often, I found myself asking Him to increase in me while I decreased. Yet, when confronted with a challenging situation, I could not get a grip on His will for me and how He wanted me to respond. But I recalled Isaiah 55:8 which states,

"For my thoughts are not your thoughts, neither are your ways my ways, saith the Lord."

So, my thing was, "Well Lord, have your way in this situation. I know of no other help! Guide me until I'm sure what it is you are trying to tell me." I began to humble myself before the Lord and seek after His desires for me rather than seeking after my desire for a changed situation. My motives were pure. I did not want to get sidetracked by petitioning God primarily for things of the world and for what I believe would work for me. I wanted to be aligned with the Spirit of God in order to get a breakthrough. I truly believe we shouldn't want anything that God doesn't desire for us to have. In Romans 8:28, we find this reassurance

"And we know that all things work together for good to them that

love God, to them who are the called according to his purpose."

This way of thinking is logical and it's Kingdom focused. Ponder this question for a moment: When we desire something that is not pleasing to Him or His will, are we better off without it? I certainly think so! I believe that all things will work out for the good. Desiring His will is much more beneficial in the long run.

I once heard my pastor, Gary Hawkins, Sr. of Voices of Faith Ministries, say, "Your outlook determines your outcome." Because I believe this statement to be true, if my outlook is "God's will" in any given situation, my outcome can only equate to "eternal blessings." Since my outlook is positive, my outcome can only be positive no matter how I look at it.

As you petition the Lord in prayer, examine your motives. Ask yourself this question. Will your desire lead to selfish gain or eternal life? Which would you prefer?

Mistake #3

Unclean Heart

CHAPTER THREE

*B*y now, I am hopeful that you understand effective prayer does not require eloquence or charm. But as Believers in Christ, we all should develop a mindset that prayer keeps us from being stuck in a box (mechanical) to one that naturally searches the heart of God for solutions. To do so, we need to ask ourselves, what's wrong with where I am now and what needs to be done to get me to where I want to be in my request and communication with God? This approach is not about ignoring our issues or problems. It's not even about pretending that they do not exist. It's about being holy when we attempt to talk with the Father and letting go of ways that are not pleasing to Him. Often we lack the willingness to deal with the reality of our sins. The truth of the matter is we quench the Holy Spirit by allowing sin to manifest and go unconfessed before making our request known to God. Therefore, this chapter deals with our disposition before the Lord.

The word of God says in Isaiah 1:15:

"And when ye spread forth your hands,
I will hide mine eyes from you: yea, when ye make many prayers,

I will not hear: your hands are full of blood"

When God is not allowed to totally manifest in our hearts through the Holy Spirit we also grieve the Spirit. Nehemiah knew this to be true; this is the reason he stated in Nehemiah 1:6:

"Let thine ear now be attentive, and thine eyes open, that thou mayest hear the prayer of thy servant, which I pray before thee now, day and night, for the children of Israel thy servants, and confess they sins of the children of Israel, which we have sinned against thee: both I and my father's house have sinned."

He took pride in how he presented himself and the Israelites to the Father.

Having a clean heart when we pray is also about staying focus on what we ultimately want to achieve, which should be... the *will of God*. As stated previously, when we aren't sure of His will, seeking God's face through the Holy Spirit for guidance is the answer. The word of God is clear about this point in Romans 8:27,

"And he that searcheth the hearts knoweth what is the mind of the Spirit, because he maketh intercession for the saints according to the will of God."

Therefore, having a cleansed heart when we pray is seeking the difference between what's wrong with where we are (sinful state) and examining what needs to be done (repentance) to be in the right mindset to petition the Father. The cost of not doing so will result in unproductive, unheard and meaningless prayers. An unclean heart will increase stress, amplify emotional bitterness and proliferate an unbalanced state of mind. The problem with most of us, and the mistake we commonly make as we go before the Lord, is that we are unwilling to release the ungodly things in our hearts. This ungodliness causes hindrances to God hearing our prayers and delays breakthrough. We put obstacles in our own way. No one has to do it; we do it to ourselves. These barriers include our unwillingness to release anger, lack of giving and receiving forgiveness, backbiting, malice, and even hatred. When will we realize that these are the very things that the devil wants us to hold and not let go? These are the very things that keep us in bondage. To avoid this, we must acknowledge the fact that the Lord is a pure and just God. He cannot and will not listen to those who serve the enemy. Granted, there are times when we don't know what to pray or when we are unsure of God's will for our lives. In addition, there are times when we can't seem to find the words to say or even how to ask things of God. But, the good news is that when we position ourselves to go before the Lord, we are reminded that He understands our hearts. He knows our desires before we ask. Also, God searches our hearts and knows the mind of the Holy Spirit who intercedes for all believers.

As we make choices to turn away from sin and immediate worldly gratification to follow after righteousness, our communication with God improves. Our communication with God will demonstrate an unprecedented time of praise and fellowship. God will begin to receive the glory.

When we pray with a clean heart, prayer is not done in a fashion that promotes bragging or lifting one's self. Rather, it is done as a means of worship to the Father in Heaven who is the sovereign Creator of all. Prayer should be done in faith and focused on Christ in order to receive His blessings. It's through faith in His words that we are delighted and take pleasure in going before Him. Without delighting in the Lord, it is impossible to have faith in Him and His word.

Let's think of it this way. When you don't have trust in someone, you don't enjoy being in their presence. You dread going to see them or even hearing their voice. You hardly want to be around them, let alone ask them for advice or guidance. The fact of the matter is, you don't find them pleasurable or worthy of *your* presence.

When you approach God with an impure heart, prayer is not exciting it is drudgery. In other words, you care less about your approach. Your only concern becomes seeking your fleshly breakthrough or an answer to your selfish prayer. This is devastating to the Lord. Can you imagine if He did us this way? Think about it for a moment. What if each time we came to the Lord in prayer, He said, "Here he/she comes again...what do you want now?"

When we are not mindful of and in tune to how we pray, we tend to approach God in a disrespectful manner. If we try to circumvent His ways and provisions, we only find ourselves lost without strength, courage, power, and blessings. Only through abiding in His words as direction for our lives, delighting in His grace and seeking after His face will we demonstrate our earnest desire to offer up fervent prayers to the Lord. When you pray, what do you reveal? Pure motives or unclean desires? You be the judge.

Mistake # 4

Misinterpretation

CHAPTER 4

*N*ormally, in communication, we strive to effectively listen to what is being said by the receiver while listening to what we are saying as the giver. Ultimately, we attempt to ensure that the receiver of our message clearly understands and listens to the message and vice versa. But often, when we think we are listening carefully, we usually grasp only half of what is said, and we retain even less. This can occur even when talking with God. Another common prayer mistake we make is we tend to hear from God what we want to hear. In other words, we hear His full message, but take in only parts of His directions or none at all. We ignore the true meaning of what He tells us. In essence, we allow our thoughts to wander and drift rather than giving attention to and concentrating on what God is saying as He addresses our requests through His words.

Let me re-emphasize what I stated in chapter 3. I'm not advocating that we must be polished or have detailed plans and be elegant and refined when we deliver our message to God. Nevertheless, we must be attentive to His voice, informal, and non-structured when communicating with Him. It should be done quietly, peacefully and without interruptions. We need to do more than just speak to the

Lord. Rather, we need to have a conversation with Him that clearly requires spending quality time in His presence, listening and meditating on His words, learning how to approach Him and understanding Him through His words. In this way, we won't misinterpret what the Lord reveals to us because we will have established a spiritual connection with Him. One of the ways that God speaks is through His word. Thus, misinterpretation can come when we are directed away from the word of God. When Satan tempted Jesus, Jesus repeatedly said, "it is written, it is written, it is written." This tells us that God's words are true and powerful. In other words, they are our covering and shield. There should be no misinterpretation of the word. If Jesus relied on them, why shouldn't we? In Ephesians 3:20 it states, "God is able to do exceedingly and abundantly above all we ask or think according to the power that works within." The power lies within God's words. Misinterpretation of the word occurs when we don't recognize His power. It also occurs when we do not acknowledge His strength. Additionally, it occurs when we do not fully put our trust in Him and allow Him to move in His own way and time. We misinterpret God's answers (His word) to our prayers by exhibiting doubt and believing worldly interpretation of our situation. We misinterpret God by going against His word , believing in things for self gratification and not Holy purification. Anytime we are lead against or away from God's word, we are misinterpreting His answers for our lives. God will not lead us away from His word, because His words are true. He said heaven and earth will pass away before His words return to Him void. If we apply this concept to our everyday lives and situations, we would be much better off. This includes our marriages, friendships, in the workplace or in social settings. It is inclusive of times when we are depressed, weak, weary and lost. God's words must be first and foremost in our lives. There are so many different kinds of prayers such as the prayer of worship, dedication, thanksgiving and change. Whatever prayer we offer up to the Lord, He desires that we are guided by His word. Knowing how to pray avoids misinterpreting His response. If you are knowledgeable about how to pray, you should know that your prayer request must be driven by the word of God. This stands to reason given His response is supported by His words. God did not leave us without His thoughts or His ways and a clear road map on how to reach Him. He made sure that everything we needed to know was documented in the book of righteousness and is supported by His grace and the Holy Spirit. As we pray, we must bask in His words and love. This is how we get our prayers answered and avoid misinterpretation. If we are driven by the word, His answers to our requests will be crystal clear. Do you see the handwriting on the wall or have you misinterpreted your answer?

Mistake #5

Underestimating the Power of Prayer

CHAPTER FIVE

*G*od's word promises that He would answer every prayer request, and I am a firm believer that He is true to His promises. As a father, this is His obligation to His children. I am also convinced that there are special provisions that He has set forth in order to have requests answered. He offers a means to avoid hindering our blessings. As stated throughout the previous chapters, God's will must be the essence of our desires. To know His will, His words must abide within us. These conditions look something like this:

- **Keep God's commandments**
  Jesus said in John 15:10, "*If ye keep my commandments*, ye shall abide in my love." This implies that we must follow after Him, His righteousness and His will. Otherwise, we are lost. Just think for a moment about a time when you started a new job. Your employer promised you certain wages for a certain amount of work (i.e., you would receive a paycheck once a week, biweekly or monthly). However, before you agreed to take the

job, there were specific job responsibilities and duties that you promised to perform in order to earn your pay. Jesus is asking us to do the same thing. He wants us to enter into an agreement or covenant with Him, if you will, in order for us to receive the promises of His blessings. Your part of this agreement is to keep His commandments and love Him for who He is. His part is to provide you, as His child, the desires of your heart.

- **Abide in Me**
  Jesus said in John 15:7, *"If ye abide in me, and my words abide in you*, ye shall ask what ye will, and it shall be done unto you."* His words should be essential elements in our daily walk throughout life's journey. His words, as our source of strength and guidance, should direct our thoughts, emotions, actions and reactions in every situation and circumstance. Everything we desire should be for the glorification of Him and His righteousness.

- **Renew Your Mind**
  Romans 12:2 states, "And be not conformed to this world: but *be ye transformed by the renewing of your mind*, that ye may prove what is that good, and acceptable, and perfect, will of God." As Christians, we should let go of all things of the flesh encompasses and place our focus on Him who created the world. We must let go and let God at all cost and remain in His perfect will.

- **Seek the Kingdom of God**
  Matthew 6:33 declares, "But *seek ye first the kingdom of God and his righteousness*; and all things shall be added unto thee." We are to pray for His will to be done, His glory and righteousness to abide in our hearts and He promises to answer. God

wants us to surrender all worldly things and thus seek after His righteousness. He wants us to confess our sins and cultivate a pure heart and cleansed souls. God is pleased and truly glorified when we seek after His righteousness. He is delighted when we ask for things that are closest to His heart.

- **Have Faith**

Hebrews 11:1 states, "**Now faith** is the substance of things hoped for, the evidence of things not seen." Similarly, II Corinthians 5:7 declares, "For we walk by faith and not by sight." Therefore, when we go to our Father in prayer, we are to pray in faith that we are in the will of God and to believe He will answer our prayers. Let's examine faith for a moment because without faith it is impossible to please Him. In Luke 9:37, Jesus and three of His disciples had just descended from the mount of transfiguration where the Son of God prayed with Moses and Elijah. Upon his arrival from the mountain, Scripture tells us Jesus was met by a man who cried out to Him, "Master, I beseech thee, look upon my son: for he is mine only child. And, lo, a spirit taketh him, and he suddenly cries out and teareth him that he foameth again, and bruising him hardly departeth from him." In other words, his son was sick and filled with evil spirits. This man also told Jesus that he asked Jesus' disciples to heal his son but they could not. Jesus immediately said to his disciples, "O faithless and perverse generation, how long shall I be with you, and suffer you?" I imagine Jesus was like, "Oh here we go! You all are so stupid! What in the world is going on?! I told you and showed you to just have faith. But I can't leave you to handle your business for one day without having to intercede. What's up with that??!! Just bring the boy to me and know that I won't always physically be here with you!!" Does this sound familiar? Honestly, Jesus' response speaks to us today. He wants us to have faith that He will do what He has promised. There is no need to see everything that will happen before it happens. Just trust in the Lord and lean not unto thy own understanding as stated in Proverbs 3:5. This is the prime example of why it is so imperative that we spend time with Him to identify and understand His will for our lives and know what He said He will do.

You know, I would be hard pressed to expect my nine and seven-year old to know what is pleasing and satisfying to me, as well as have faith in me if I never spent quality time talking, listening, playing and praying with them. In today's society, we are so caught up in the hustle and bustle of life that we fail to recognize how valuable quality time is for ourselves and the ones we love most. Nowadays, we place our young ones in front of the television and expect them to be taught the lessons of life and everything we want them to know. We don't pray with them, we don't eat with them, nor do we sit with them just to listen and discuss the excitement and challenges of their day. God is asking us to do otherwise with Him. He wants us to establish a prayer closet and dedicate quality time with Him so that, before we even request from Him, we first understand Him. In this way, we will be aligned with the desires of His heart. We will be connected in Spirit and want what He wants.

He wants to answer every prayer request of man, but first and foremost, He desires our hearts. God wants us to have faith in Him and earnestly seek after His righteousness for His name's sake. He wants us to have faith in His promises, just as He expected from His disciples when He quieted the storm. In Matthew 8:23-26, it states

"And, when he was entered into a ship,
his disciples followed him. And, behold, there arose

a great tempest in the sea, insomuch that the ship was covered with the waves: but he was asleep. And his disciples came to him, and awoke him, saying, Lord, save us: we perish. And he saith unto them, Why are ye fearful, O ye of little faith?"

He wants us to believe in Him in our hearts because His words and promises are true. There is truly power in our prayers to Him when we align ourselves with His righteousness. In Matthew 21:21-22, Jesus says to His disciples,

"Verily, I say unto you, if ye have faith, and doubt not, ye shall not only do this which is done to the fig tree, but also if ye shall say unto the mountain, Be thou removed, and be thou cast into the sea; it shall be done. And all things, whatsoever ye shall ask in prayer, believing, ye shall receive."

In summary, *faith in Christ is like walking hand in hand with the Father through belief; it is being unable to see the future, yet having the determination to trust and remain with Him until the end of time despite the unknown.*

As you begin to spend time with the Father, you will know the truth in His promises as the Holy Spirit reveals understanding and wisdom in your heart. You must ask yourself, "Could His words abide in me if I never seek to discover them? Am I holding up my end of the bargain? And, what is my relationship with the Most High? Is He just a supernatural existence or reality deep in my soul? The answer to these questions will move you closer to the crucial meaning of faith.

The Father that created the world and the things in it doesn't want to be treated like a "sugardaddy." In other words, He doesn't want to be treated like someone you use when you want them to fulfill your desires, only to be dropped like a hot potato. God's love is so perfect and much greater than any man can imagine. Just think He gave His only begotten Son to die for our sins so that we can have eternal life. He doesn't want us to be surprised or marveled about what He can do. He has given us His promises clearly in His word. If we are abiding in His word and He is in us, we very well know what He will do. Scripture teaches that nothing is too impossible or too hard for God. So, what are you waiting on? Who will you trust? Will it be man? Or will it be God?

Mistake #6

Taking Rejection the Wrong Way

CHAPTER SIX

*I*n previous chapters, I discussed certain provisions to God's answers to our prayers. Now that we know the Father will answer our prayers, within this chapter, I want to focus on another common prayer mistake which is how our response to God's answers hinders effective prayers.

There will be times when it seems like your prayers are unanswered based on several factors. First, when you pray, there will be times when you have been faithful and done all you can do in a situation. You wait and wait. Yet, it seems like God will not answer your prayer. You even encourage others in the midst of your waiting. You lose strength while waiting. However, instead of becoming negative, you hold on and you are encouraged by the fact that God will answer your prayers. Despite the facts that He will do so in His own time and not yours. Secondly, we may ask God for things that are not in His will and thirdly, God's answer maybe no or even different than our expectations in an effort to get the glory, honor and praise He desires.

God's answer sometimes will be no or different than your expectations

I recall back in my twenties praying to God to marriage a certain man (actually, several different men) because I thought I was in love. God said no to these requests, because He knew my soul mate and knew my future. Today, I thank Him eminently because had God given me those particular desires, which in fact, was not His will, I wouldn't have the wonderful husband I have today.

I also remember getting pregnant twice out of wedlock. I could not understand for the life of me why God would not allow me to birth these children. I remember asking Him why. But today, I thank Him for His omnipotent power to have me to spontaneously abort (miscarry) those children. Again, God knew I wasn't strong enough to not only carry the children, but to care for myself.

I also recall petitioning the Lord for certain jobs. I don't know about you, but I use to ask God for a particular job that *I* thought would be right for me based on what I saw within myself. I did not consider the fact that He knew how much I could handle in a given situation. While I thought these jobs were best suited for me and I them, God denied these requests as well. At the time, I did not see it as simple as that. But God knew what was best for me. I saw things from the perspective that I wasn't worthy or desired these positions, when in fact, had He given them to me, I could have been layoff or terminated based on my bad attitude. The point I'm trying to make is you must thank God for answering your prayers in His way. This may very well mean that sometimes God's answer will be no. But because of who God is, we should be grateful and worship Him for being omnipresence, omniscience and omnipotent. He knows all and is all knowing. Because of this, we should not make the mistake of getting angry with God for His decisions. But begin to thank Him for looking out for our best interest. We should pray for His will to be done because He has all power in His hands. I now look at things from the perspective that if it is His will for me to receive a desire, I gladly accept it and appreciate His answer. However, if He chooses not to give me a certain desire, at a specified time I delight myself in Him because He ultimately is giving me the desires of my heart (which in essence, is His heart). We must put His desires first and then we will receive His best and even when we don't, He still blesses us. Isn't that the best way to receive? Again, we should not want anything God does not want us to have, no matter what or who it is. This is why we should put our total trust in Him and seek Him for guidance. Guess what? If we do not, we will be lost. We should seek God for all things and trust Him enough to know He can and will make the right decision on our behalf. We should not get bent out of shape because we did not receive something we believe was for our good. We should set our minds on believing in what God has for us and not on the depths of our desires.

Don't get me wrong, God will answer each and every prayer request and bless you with your desires...in His time, in His ways. But in order to grow in grace, we must change our stance, outlook and perspective regarding what we request, how we request it, and how we respond to God's answers.

God answers in His time, not yours

I want to use for an illustration Abraham, Mary and Martha to make a point about God's timing. In the Old Testament, Abraham and Sarah desperately wanted to bear a child of their own. While God promised Abraham that He would bless them with a child, God did not do so until Abraham was one hundred years old and Sarah was ninety-nine (*God's timing, not theirs*). Now, I don't know about you but if I had to wait that many years to have a prayer answered, I would begin to feel that my prayer request would not be fulfilled to develop a sense of rejection to my request. Wouldn't you? I would probably begin to tell the Lord, "Well, I guess I'm not going to have any children, "or ask why me Lord?" When God doesn't answer when you want Him to, do you begin to think negatively and doubt that His blessings and promises will ever manifest in your life? Well, I must admit, sometimes I begin to think how I can get what I want versus waiting patiently on the Lord. In the case with Abraham and Sarah, I truly mean waiting patiently on the Lord. Let's take a look at the Scriptures in Genesis 15:2-5,

"But Abram said, "Lord God, what wilt thou give me, seeing I go childless and the steward of my house is this Eliezer of Damascus?" And Abram said, "Behold to me thous hast given no seed: and, lo, one born in my house in mine heir."

"And, behold, the word of the Lord came unto him, saying, This shall not be thine heir; but he that shall come forth out of thine own bowels shall be thine heir. And he brought him forth abroad, and said, Look now toward heaven, and tell the stars, if thou be able to number them: and he said unto him, So shall they seed be."

Genesis 17:17-19 states,

"Then Abraham fell upon his face, and laughed, and said in his heart, Shall a child be born unto him that is a hundred years old? And shall Sarah, that is ninety year old bear? And Abraham said unto God, O that Ishmael might live before thee! And God said, Sarah thy wife shall bear thee a son indeed; and thou shalt call his name Isaac: and I will establish my covenant with him for an everlasting covenant, and with his seed after him."

As you can see, Abraham wanted a child at the time of his request to the Father. This is just like us. We want things when we want them, exactly how we want them, and when we want them.

And sometimes we are like Abraham, we begin to analyze things. Abraham analyzed his age, Sarah's age, the viability of her womb, etc. We also begin to put things into our own perspective....the way we see it. But, God promised Abraham a son. However, at the same time, Scripture shows us that Abraham in his own wisdom thought God's timing was off. He thought it would be somewhat crazy for him to father a child at one hundred and for Sarah to give birth at ninety-nine. Sarah even laughed to herself when she learned that she was going to bear a child at that age. However, Abraham did not lose faith in the Lord's promises. Romans 4:19-21 describes him (his faith) in this way:

"And being not weak in faith, he considered not his own body now dead, when he was about a hundred years old, neither yet the deadness of Sarah's womb. He staggered not at the promise of God through unbelief; but was strong in faith, giving glory to God; And being fully persuaded that, what he had promised, he was able also to perform."

Therefore, you see this was God's plan. Ultimately, He answered Abraham's prayer, but God did so in His own time. Hence, in Genesis 21:5-6 it states,

"Now Abraham was a hundred years old, when his son Isaac was born unto him."

Consequently, we must be like Abraham. We must remember the promises of the Lord and hold on to His every word. Because of God's love through the Holy Spirit, He is an on time God and will never disappoint us.

Before we examine John chapter 11, in which Jesus raised Lazarus from the dead in His own time, I want to re-emphasize and make it clear that we must have faith and believe that God's promises will become reality. God doesn't promise the *when*, He does promise the *what*.

Mary and Martha, sisters of Lazarus, sent for Jesus and informed Him of Lazarus' condition. However, Jesus did not come running immediately although He loved Mary, Martha and Lazarus. He stayed where he was for two additional days. During this time, Scripture teaches us that Lazarus died. Once Jesus arrived, He told Martha to remove the stone where Lazarus was buried. Nevertheless, Martha said to Him, there would be a stench because Lazarus had been dead for four days. Now, remember, Mary and Martha sent for Jesus four days prior, but Jesus chooses to come in His time. The reason for the delay was for God to get the glory when Jesus raised Lazarus from the dead. Jesus knew many people would be around when He performed the miracle. With the crowd watching, Jesus told Lazarus to get up and Lazarus rose from the dead. As you can see, the Lord delivers and does so right on time.

Did you notice, that neither Abraham, Sarah, Mary or Martha got bent out of shape because of God's timing? So, I ask you, which would you prefer: your time or the Lord's?

Mistake #7

Not Listening to our Request

CHAPTER SEVEN

As I write this book, I'm reminded of how valuable my conversations are and relationship is with my heavenly Father. I embrace His Holy Spirit, for without the Lord in my life right now, I truly don't know what I would do. I bless and reverence His Holy name. Sometimes we can make a request to our Father without really realizing or understanding the meaning of the request. For instance, for the past seven months my husband has been deployed with the Armed Forces and serving his country on a military base away from our home state. Now, this is during the season where we as a country experienced a war. Many soldiers fell to their deaths and the possibility of others returning home was bleak. Initially, I asked the Lord to bring him back home and not take him away from his family because the children and I needed him. Even friends would say to me, let's pray and ask the Lord to bring him home. Well, seven months thereafter, my husband received orders to report to his command station. His tour of duty extended from six months to a year. Now, I don't know about you, but for me this was a hard pill to swallow. I believed that if I continuously prayed for God to bring my husband home, Marvin would not fulfill the desires the

Lord planned for his life. I had to change my mindset and begin to seek God's face for His desire not only in this situation but so that I could clearly understand the message, God was trying to send to me. It did not dawn on me until months later that I had also been praying for a closer relationship with my heavenly Father. I had been praying that God would give me strength to lean on Him through all my trials and tribulations. I did not realize that while Marvin was present, I would seek his advice and wisdom before the Lord's. This was not what God wanted me to do. God had to put in my life a gap and void that could not be closed except through Him.

As I continued to deal with this situation, I learned that life in and of itself throws blows and curves that are so unpredictable that you must have faith to endure. But there's something about knowing the Father and asking for His guidance in your life. I had to call on Him and worship Him during these times. Sometimes, my speaking to Him was like a moan. Words did not come out of my mouth. My heart ached and all I wanted from the Lord was for Him to hold me in His arms and rock me like a mother would a child. Sometimes even when I wanted to ask for a specific thing, I couldn't. My eyes would fill up with water and I wanted everything to go away. At the same time, I wanted to be obedient to the will of God for Marvin and my family. I did not want to ask God for something He did not want us to have. I wanted God's will to be done and not my selfish desires. However, I remember what the Lord told me. He wanted me to solely depend on Him. He wanted me to trust Him, to understand that He would bring me out, and give me strength as I endured the pain. He told me to testify of His goodness and power. He wanted to show me peace that surpasses all understanding, even during difficult moments. For that, I bless Him for the experience of being separated from my husband. Even when I didn't mumble a word, He knew my heart. He read my heart and knew exactly how I was feeling. This is why having a solid relationship with the Father and asking for His will to be done is so important. God will put you in a situation where there is nowhere else to turn, but to Him. I bless Him because during this time it has brought me closer to the Lord than ever before. I thank Him for the communication we have had with one another. God will avail Himself to be loved and to provide love and strength. He places His children in positions where they cannot call on anyone but Him.

I remember how I would call on friends or they would call me, but it did not seem to be enough. No matter how hard they tried to comfort me, it was not enough. We would pray or they would offer prayers, but it still was not enough, because my focus in prayer was on the wrong thing. My mindset was not on what God would have for me, but it was on what I wanted for myself. People would say, I will keep you and your family in my prayers, but that still did not do it. They would say be strong, Gayle, you know the Word, but those words did not help me. It was not until "I" truly surrendered and searched the heart of the Lord for myself. "I" had to call on the name of JESUS!!! "I" had to bless Him and believe that what God had for me was wonderful and awesome! "I" challenge you; if you are going through any difficulties in life, bless Him today. Seek after Him and His words. Bless the Lord with your heart no matter what you are going through. I challenge you to praise your way through your situation. This is the time to just praise the Lord with a loud voice and begin to magnify His Name. Begin to tell Him how wonderful He has been and declare to Him you are nothing without His presence in your life. Trust that He will deliver you and lead you in the path of righteousness for your overall betterment. Desire a relationship that brings you closer to Him.

So many times when I'm down and feeling low (yes, I love the Lord, but do feel like my back is up against a wall at times) God fills me with His Holy Spirit to mold and make me into what He wants me to be. He continuously waits on me to come to Him and allow Him to give me exactly what I need versus what I want. His plan has already been established, but He allows me to seek Him to carry His plan by allowing me to go through trials and tribulations. Believe me; this only brings closeness to the Father. He tells me to hold on to my faith in Him while His grace surrounds me. He sends Angels from Heaven to keep watch over me as stated in Psalm 91. Blessed be the name of the Lord on High! I challenge you to listen to your request. Make sure you are in the will of God. Make sure you are not asking something of Him for selfish gain. What are your requests today?

Mistake #8

Getting Distracted

CHAPTER EIGHT

I think by now that you know if you expect God to answer your prayers, you must abide in His will. Since His will centers on His righteousness, He definitely has a strong desire to bless those who follow His heart and walk upright in His grace. He yearns to fulfill every desire, want and need because His words dictate this as reality. Matthew 6:33 states,

"But seek ye first the kingdom of heaven and his righteousness; and all these things shall be added unto you."

However, often people are filled with distractions that cause God's blessings and His will to be hindered and forfeited in their lives. Let's look at David who was appointed King of Israel by the Lord and Bathsheba. The story takes place during the spring, when kings traditionally went off to war. However, David sent his army to fight a war while he stayed back in Jerusalem. Now, the first question that comes to my mind is why would a king stay at home and send his troops off to fight? Can you see the initial distraction? At any rate, II Samuel 11:1, tells us one night David got out of his bed and walked on a roof top where he saw Bathsheba bathing. Now, mind you, Bathsheba was a married woman and her husband, Uriah was sent to war with the other soldiers. Now, whether Bathsheba intentionally bathed so that David or others could see her is still a mystery. The Bible does not specify. However, it does state that David saw her and, as stated in II Samuel 11:2, she was beautiful. As a result, David called for his spies to find out about Bathsheba. Their report revealed that she was a married woman. The yearning of lust and passion magnified David's desire to have an affair with Bathsheba, and so he did. After the sexual encounter between the two adulterous lovers, David did not stop there. He had Uriah murdered after he found out that Bathsheba was pregnant. While David repented for his sin, God showed no mercy on David and Bathsheba. It came to pass, that the birth of their child, conceived out of wedlock, would end in death.

Do you ever wonder why David did what he did? Well, David was distracted by lust and illicit of passion. He took his eyes off of the Lord for the sake of self gratification. He possessed the wrong motives. As a result, the blessing of a child turned tart. Although this story ends happily with the birth of Solomon, the blessings of the Lord can be delayed, stalled or even cancelled if repentance and remorse are not displayed from one's heart to the Lord.

Let's examine other Bible characters who allowed the distractions of lies, control and deception to hinder their blessings. Acts 4 tells us of how believers prayed and the Holy Spirit was upon them. No one at that time lacked for anything. They brought things they possessed and the price of things sold to the Apostles to give to others. However, in Acts 5:3, there was a man by the name of Ananias and his wife, Sapphira, who did the contrary.

*"But Peter said, Ananias why hath Satan filled thine heart
to lie to the Holy Ghost, and to keep back part of the price
of the land?"*

Ananias, as Scripture stated, lied to God (not man) after Peter questioned him regarding the sale of his land. Ananias dropped dead as a result of his decision. His wife Sapphira was soon tested to see which route she would take in this situation. Three hours later, Peter questioned her regarding the amount of money received from the sale of their land. Now, at the time, she was not aware Ananias had died. So, when the question was posed to her, she to decided to lie as well. Consequently, she also died and was buried next to her husband.

Time and time again, people think they are getting away with dishonesty, deception and being a con, but truth be told, God knows all. I Corinthians 2:10-11 states,

*"But God hath revealed them unto us by his Spirit: for the Spirit
searcheth all things, yea, the deep things of God."*
*"For what man knoweth the things of a man, save the spirit of man
which is in him? even so the things of God knoweth no man,
but the Spirit of God."*

In essence, while God gives us the ability to make decisions, there are consequences to all decisions made outside the will of God. When we come in prayer to the Lord, we must eliminate these desires and behaviors from our hearts through the Holy Spirit. Deceitfulness speaks to one's character. If your character is focused on fraudulence, lying, dishonesty and corruption, your eyes are not on the Lord. Therefore, you are distracted; the Holy Spirit is limited, which in turn impedes your ability to receive blessings and hear from the Lord.

Webster defines "distract" as, "to turn aside, to draw or direct (as one's attention) to a different object or in different direction at the same time. To stir up or confuse with conflicting emotions or motives." Doesn't this definition reflect the position most people are in when they are not lead by the Father? When their eyes are on self and off glory and righteousness? But watch this, often, these same people pray and expect the same results and outcomes as those who earnestly seek Him and live by God's words. They pray out of routine, practice, yet never factor in the distractions of malice, contempt, control, envy and any other ill-gotten things that exist in their hearts. Do these things sound like the will of God? As stated earlier, if we expect God to answer our prayers, we must walk in His will. What I mean is this: God's words must abide in our hearts. We must embed His ways in our spirits. The ways of Satan do not please or impress God-or is God willing to listen or bless our mess! God views anything that is not of good rapport, pure, humble, meek, honest, and righteous as distractions to receiving blessings and hearing His voice. People further hinder prayers when they do not live holy lives.

Let's further examine how prayers are hindered in the book of Ezra. God fulfilled His promise to Israel by bringing them back to their land after seventy years of captivity. Ezra was a scribe or interpreter of the Law. Ezra returned to Jerusalem to find his people engaging in intermarriage with other cultures and religions (mixed marriages). They were living a life of unholiness and ungodliness. Ezra 9:1 tells us how shocked and amazed Ezra was at the existence of such acts. He began to pray to the Lord for forgiveness of the people because he knew how displeased his Father would be. God saw the land as "unclean and filthy."

"Now these things were done, the prince came to me, saying,

The people of Israel, and the priests, and the Levites, have not separated themselves from the people of the lands, doing according to their abominations, even of the Canaanites, the Hittites, the Perizzites, the Jebusites, the Ammonites, the Moabites, the Egyptians, and the Amorites."

Because the people married foreign women, they were dealt with based on the decision they made. Thank God, Ezra sought the Lord in prayer for the people of Israel. Also, thank God the people of Israel decided to follow the laws of the Father. The whole point here is that when people live according to what man has created and not the Lord, destruction occurs. I truly believe this is one of the reasons why we have many illnesses, diseases and mishaps in today's society. There are so many people living their lives according to man-made religions, groups and ungodly customs. People who constantly live according to man are some of the same individuals who pray to our Father even though they have non-repentful spirits. They pray, but refuse to live according to God's ways. I have come to tell you that God has declared that those living in a non-repentant state have detestable prayers. Therefore, even when these people pray to the Lord, it puts a bitter taste in His mouth. Let me show you why I say this. Proverbs 28:9 states,

"He that turneth away his ear from hearing the law, even his prayer shall be abomination."

Look! These are God's words, not mine! This reality has to hurt if you fall into this category. Unfortunately, if people who choose to live their lives in ways that do not line up with the words of the Lord, they are condemned. God doesn't pay any attention to the words that are uttered out of the mouths of those choosing to consistently live in sin. As mentioned in chapter 3, this is referred to as quenching the Holy Spirit. Only when repentance takes place will God hear from us. Let me show you another reason I am making this point. God also points out in Proverbs 15:8, 15:29, and John 9:31 respectively, the following:

"The sacrifice of the wicked is an abomination to the Lord: but the prayer of the upright is his delight."

"The Lord is far from the wicked but he heareth the prayer of the righteous."

"Now we know that God heareth not sinners: but if any man be a worshipper of God, and doeth his will, him he heareth."

These Scriptures suggest to me that those living an ungodly life are far removed from the Lord until they repent. He views these distractions as wicked. He does not hear them, acknowledge, or bless them unless they repent and turn from their sinful ways. He wants His people to live a life that is upright and holy. Those who are not, or choose not to, will not inherit the Kingdom of Heaven nor God's perfect plan for their lives no matter what sacrifices they make. He will ignore their voices.

God tells us to come as we are. He loves to hear from those who repent of their sins and who ask forgiveness to receive a change of heart, mind and soul. Matthew 21:22 teaches us that in all things, whatsoever ye shall ask in prayer, believing, ye shall receive. A sinner's prayer is where one evolves from a sinful state to a mindset of a "willing and obedient heart" that glorifies God first. God looks for sinners to have a pure heart before asking things of Him. In this way, the distractions are released and the focus is now on Christ. God wants us to pray continuously so that He will order our steps, tongues, minds and ultimately our hearts. This includes anger, disputing and doing wrong to others. 1 Timothy 2:8 states,

"I will therefore that men pray every where, lifting up holy hands, without wrath and doubting."

These scriptures confirm that God is the ruler of all and the giver of all things. He wants to bless His people. He wants us to let go of the distractions and concentrate on His righteousness. These conditions must be present in our lives to receive God's blessings. What are your distractions? Is it man? Or are you focused on God?

Mistake #9

Praying with a Limit

CHAPTER NINE

*T*he Bible invites us and actually commands us to pray, and to
do so endlessly. Scripture says in I Thessalonians 5:17 to pray
without ceasing. Luke 18:1 also states,

> *"And he spake a parable unto them, this end, that men ought*
> *always to pray, and not to faint."*

These scriptures mean that we must always be ready to pray. We
must always have a willing heart to go before the throne of grace to
praise, worship, request, and hear from the Lord. One of our
mistakes is that we like to put God on the back burner. We like to go
to Him every now and then. These actions are more prevalent when
we hurt.

So, let me ask a few questions to get you to think about your
situation. Do you ever wonder where God is when you hurt? Better
yet, who is the first person or what is the first thing you turn to
when you suffer or feel alone? You know, each day thousands of
people face sorrows, pain and tragedy. Loved ones pass away,
marriages die, layoffs increase and dreams of security vanish. As

people continue to live, everyone will experience situations that are traumatic and will change their lives forever. Tragedy has no color or racial boundaries. It is something that is a part of the world's daily existence. Those who suffer traumatic experiences feel hurt and helplessness. They can lose all hope during their place of pain. Those who struggle to cope with the effects of trauma will need a person to be open and sensitive.

Let me assure you, in such times people seek help, comfort, assurance, and safety. In moments of tragedy and crisis there is no better place to turn than to our God who has promised to help those who seek Him in times of trouble. The Christian response to tragedy of any proportion, whether it is the collapse of great towers or the collapse of a marriage, should model after Jesus Christ's examples and answers. I'm sure we all have asked the question, "Lord why is this happening to me?" As children of God, addressing the question of causation of suffering, we should avoid taking people back to figuring out the cause of their pain. Instead, we should try to lead them to a fervent prayer life. Many may think that they suffer because of something they have done in the past, but Scripture shows us that this is not the case per se. In II Timothy 3:12, we are told that Believers in Christ will be persecuted if they seek Him. It states,

"Yea, and all that will live godly in Christ Jesus shall suffer persecution."

Christ Himself suffered pain and suffering for our sins, as I Peter 4:12-13 indicates,

"Beloved, think it not strange concerning the fiery trial which is to try you, as though some strange thing happened unto you: But rejoice, inasmuch as ye are partakers of Christ's sufferings; that,

when his glory shall be revealed, ye may be glad also with exceeding joy."

As Christians, we won't always have an answer as to why suffering occurs. But as Believers in Christ Jesus, we do know God is all powerful and sovereign. He holds the power, and sometimes He allows things to happen to people for they're good. In Luke 13:1-5, Jesus was asked by some people what did he think about the tragedy that had just struck the city. They wanted to know how Jesus dealt with the current issue and why the tragedy occurred. Jesus responded by saying in Luke 13:2-3,

"Suppose ye that these Galileans were sinners above all the Galileans, because they suffered such things? I tell you, Nay: but, except ye repent, ye shall all likewise perish."

Jesus redirected their thinking. He was more interested in giving life and hope than the critics who wanted to point fingers of blame at innocent victims.

During traumatic times, Christians should also strive to be like Jesus. We should direct others to pray and encourage those who suffer. We should attempt to focus on life and hope. We should redirect mind-sets from thinking about the cause and "why"of illness or death, to how the situation can produce value. It can strengthen perseverance or steadiness by allowing a person to totally focus on God through constant prayer. These are reasons we should not pray with a limit. Prayer should be a constant way of life.

I say all of this to stress, prayer should come naturally during times of dilemma, death, tragedy, and pain. If we constantly pray, seeking the Lord becomes a natural reaction when we become challenged and face hardship. The more we pray, the more we will find it to be our greatest weapon when we experience trials and tribulations.

Prayer should not be a time when we babble on and on and run off at the mouth just to be heard. But prayer should be non-stop from the standpoint that it is fervent and emanates a heart seeking after the Father. We should not wait until the hour of trouble to seek the Lord in prayer. Doing so puts a limit on your prayer time. Prayer should be the first thing we do each and every morning God's grace awakens us. Prayers should continuously be in our mouths throughout the day and again at night. This is especially true when we are awaken during early morning hours like three or four a.m. Ephesians 6:18 states,

"Praying always with all prayer and supplication in the Spirit, and watching thereunto with all perseverance and supplication for all saints."

Not only does God want us to pray for ourselves, He also expects us to pray for others. Prayer delights the heart of the Father. The more we do it, the more we grow in grace and learn of His will and ways. When we pray for others, whether we know exactly what to say or not, we must first realize that the person who grieves and faces tragedy will have to deal with their true feelings as well. However, a common belief about loss is that unless you have been through it yourself you really can't understand how someone else is feeling. But, as children of God, we can encourage those who grieve to have hope and pray. We can convey that in the midst of tragedy, there is still hope because God has promised never to leave us or to forsake us. When nothing makes sense and leaders are confused or frustrated, God has the answers. Jesus said, "Lo, I am with you always, even unto the end of the world." This means we must first look to the hills from which our help comes. We must pray and persistently seek guidance from the Lord. As we constantly pray, we must also sit back and listen to the voice of the Lord. Some people do more talking than listening. Remember, prayer is communication with

God. It is a two-way process. Sometimes you got to cry and just listen to the guidance the Lord provides. It is okay to cry and share your deepest feelings to the Lord. We should remember the story of Lazarus. When Lazarus died, Scripture tells us two words, "Jesus wept." If Jesus himself cried out of hurt, loss and grief, why shouldn't we?

We must be persistent in our prayers just like the widow in Luke 18:1-5. In this parable, Jesus explains there was a judge in the city that did not fear God or man. A widow went to him asking for protection from her enemies; however, for a while he would not pay her any attention. Because of her persistence, the judge granted her request. Jesus later explained that if the man, who did not fear the Lord, would avenge the widow's, would not God who is almighty and has all power do the same and more for His children who call upon Him consistently.

We must go before the throne of grace as often as Jesus did to communicate with the Father. Each and every time before Jesus began a mission, He would pray to His Father. He consistently took time out to talk with God. If praying was that important to our King, doesn't it stand to reason we should follow suit? Jesus prayed all night and then selected His disciples based on His communion with the Father. He took enough time with the Father to find out who should walk with Him and be on His team.

There are 1440 minutes in a day. How many minutes do you use for prayer?

Mistake #10

Not Listening When God Speaks

CHAPTER TEN

*I*n order to have prayers answered, one must recognize the voice
of the One who answers prayer requests. Have you ever recog-
nized the voice of the Lord and knew exactly what He instructed
you to do, but you chose to do the total opposite of what He said?
Or, have you ever experienced a time when you knew the Lord was
speaking to you through someone? He told you exactly which way
to turn, how to react, precisely what to say, and you still did what
your heart wanted to do. You ultimately found yourself in a world
of trouble and turmoil. In addition, do you find it ironic that when
we get ourselves in these predicaments the first person we run back
to is God? The One who told us what to do in the first place? Does
that make sense? Well, you see, another prayer mistake we make is
we ask God for guidance yet, when we get an answer, we throw it
right out the window as though we are clueless to His response.

As I stated in chapter 5, God promises He will answer every
prayer request. You can be sure of that. He will speak to you loudly
and clearly as though you can see the words coming right out of His
mouth. And trust me, when He answers, trust me, you will surely

know. Isaiah 30:21 states,

"And thine ears shall hear a word behind thee, saying, This is the way, walk ye in it, when ye turn to the right hand, and when ye turn to the left."

Now, do not get me wrong, sometimes we doubt the things we do not understand. But we must remember, God's words teaches us that He cares so much for us that He listens and answers prayers of His people. Meaning, God will direct our path if we listen. If we believe God's words are true, that they will never leave His mouth and return void and that Heaven and earth shall pass away before His words are made out to be a lie, then why can't we see how He will guide, lead, and direct us in the proper way to go? The challenge many of us face is that we are so consumed with wanting to do what we believe is right in order to achieve what we consider "true happiness." In other words, we want to do our own thing. We want to seek God on a part-time basis. We want to give Him part-time employment. You know how that works. When a person works part-time, they are not full-time equivalent employees; they only work on an as needed basis. Nevertheless, the good news is God remains merciful that even when we kick Him to the curb and do not always want Him around, He still wants us to choose Him in every way and at every opportunity. He wants us to commit to His ways with every decision, every word that proceeds out of our mouth, every thought, and every reaction and response. That is awesome!

Just think what it will be like if God was anything like man. Do you truly believe He would stick around? Not! I don't think so! We see that everyday at home, at the work place, even in church. We try our best not to bother those who seem like they do not want to be bothered. But look at God! When we try to push Him away, we treat Him this way, He still promises to direct us and give us joy. Look at that. We treat Him like nothing, and He *Gives* us joy. What an awesome God we serve. Proverb 3:6 states,

> *"In all thy ways acknowledge Him, and He shall*
> *direct your paths."*

What a magnificent God to serve!

In order for God to do what He has promised, we must hold up our end of the bargain. We must seek His face and His righteousness, and abide in His will. This is the only way we will be able to hear the true voice. I know some of you are like me in saying, "Yeah, but how do I get there?" Well, let's us use difficult times again as an example because we all have them. If you are anything like me, our concept of a difficult time is when all hell breaks loose and it's one thing after another. These are the times when people start to question your ability and talk down about you. Eventually you start to question your own ability to do things just because someone else has said you are incapable. People start getting sick around you, your close friends (those you thought were, anyway) start to turn their backs on you. They just don't seem to get it anymore. It's when your spouse starts acting down right crazy! Your children begin to be disobedient and won't listen to your directions. These are times when you wonder what else could possibly go wrong. I do not know about you, but I have questioned God. I have said things like, "God, what in the world is going on? Do you hear my cries; are you listening to me, Lord?" When will you deliver me out of this mess?"

When you were in personal crisis, did you ever feel God was unavailable? Did you feel you had nowhere to turn? When you called a friend, were they always available? When they were available, did you always feel safe, secure and know that they had the right answers? Did you feel they were able to turn your situation around? Personally, I can think of plenty of times when my faith in the Lord was not that strong. I can think of numerous times when I just wanted to give up. Actually, I did give up in some instances. God could have been speaking to me, but I did not hear Him. I did not always put God first in all things. I still don't sometimes, and God forbid if I did not repent for it. I truly believe that when we ask Him these questions of uncertainty, we are operating in the flesh. Our minds are not on the anointing that He so graciously provided to us. When we operate in the flesh, we think like those who don't serve a true and living God. This displeases our Father. As a result, we cannot hear Him when he is speaking because we seek personal happiness first to fill a sense of comfort and security in life. Rather, we should first seek the kingdom of God and His will for our lives. When we allow our goals obtaining happiness surpass the desire to serve the Lord, we experience a sense of loss, disconnection and unnecessary pain. However, if we earnestly seek to hear the voice of the Lord, through praying, fasting and studying His word, God promises He will give us unspeakable joy and peace. It's the kind of peace that you find difficult to explain. This is why we must change our attitudes and mindsets to reach one endpoint being Christ-like and Christ-centered. This requires submission to the Father's will which in essence rejects the primary goal in life of being happy. It means doing what Jesus did sitting and meditating on the Lord. It means being lead by the Holy Spirit and listening to the voice of the Most High.

God wants and strongly desires for us to be content in all things. But first and foremost, He wants our attention and hearts to be focused on things that would exemplify the fruits of the spirit (i.e., love, peace, longsuffering, kindness, goodness, faithfulness, gentleness and self-control). If these things exist in us when we are faced with misfortune, difficulties, trouble and hardship, our actions will exhibit the core existence of the Savior living in us. We will not respond the way others respond who are not serving Him. Rather, we will immediately be reminded that all things are in the Father's hand. We will also acknowledge that all things work out for the good according to God's purpose. We become familiar with His will and His voice.

Often, people have wrong ideas about what it takes to obtain personal happiness. I say this because most people's general ideal or concept of happiness centers around worldly possessions such as wealth, success, homes, cars, power, authority, recognition, spouses/mates, jobs, and security, to name a few. However, Romans 12:2 teaches us that we should not be conformed to the things of this world. Yet, we put all of our hope in these things and expect them to bring us happiness. In fact, we put these things before the Lord who is the true giver of contentment.

Listening to God when He speaks means we are comfortable and content with receiving His guidance and directions. It means we abide in the spirit of the Lord for directions in our life. But guess what? We are the only ones who can decide what we will or will not do. God will direct us as far as we allow Him to. When we allow ourselves to let God speak to our hearts and circumstances, we actually say to Him and ourselves that we have a committed heart, a renewed mind and a willingness to be lead by Him. In that, we tend to spend more time with Him, abiding and remaining in His presence. As we do these things, our faith increases and our fleshly desires decrease. We become more in tune with His promises and witness the incredible power that He holds as it manifests itself in our lives. Who are you listening to?

Conclusion

*G*od is Faithful and just. He will do everything that He has promised. God wants to bless His people in ways that we cannot begin to imagine. He wants to provide us with the desires of our hearts and fill us with the riches of Heaven just as He attempted to do with Adam and Eve. However, God demands certain things from His people. He demands that we live according to His ways. He demands that we walk in righteousness and live by the Holy Spirit. He demands that we let our light shine so that others can see His good works in us, especially during times of trials and tribulations. God demands that He is first and not last. He demands that our lives line up with His Spirit and His will. He demands that we seek His Kingdom first. He demands that we put off the ways of man and follow Him. God expects us to receive what we ask in His name. He expects us to repent of our sins and walk according to His commandments. He expects us to know He is God and that He has all power in His hands. He expects us to lead others to Him so that the Kingdom of God can be ours. He expects us to seek after His Heart and constantly abide by His words. He expects a constant line of communication to be a priority in our life so that He can lead, guide and direct His people. God expects a two-way partnership with us and He will deliver **RIGHT ON TIME!**

If you have not given your life to the Lord, I ask you to repeat these words:

Father, I believe with my heart that Jesus is Lord and I believe that you raised Him from the dead. Father, I am a sinner and want you to come into my life. Please cleanse me of all of my transgressions. Please take over my life so that I may serve you and only you Lord. I ask these many blessings in your Son Jesus' name. Amen.

Quick Reference Summary

Chapter Three-Mistake #3
Unclean Heart

Chapter Four-Mistake #4
Misinterpretation

Chapter Five-Mistake #5
Underestimating the Power of Power

Chapter Ten-Mistake #10
Not Listening When God Speaks

Printed in the United States
25811LVS00006B/190-510

9 781597 810081